POWER 2 LIVE

THROUGH OBSTACLES

by **Oliver Adams**
#Coach

OLIVER ADAMS

#Coach

ParaMind Publications

Library of Congress Control Number: 2018939584
ISBN 978-0-9979870-9-6
Printed in the United States of America

Dedication

Every day I consider myself blessed, more importantly my children comes to mind. I dedicate this book "Power 2 Live Through Obstacles" to my children James Adams, Nyah Adams my nephew Maurice Tillman and my grandson Hendrix Oliver Adams.

Anyone that makes a promise to friends and family should climb mountains to make sure that promise is kept. Oliver is that man for me and countless others.

Tammy Noll, President-Elect

2018 Women's Council Of REALTORS, Georgia

****

Favorite Song to acknowledge My Mothers Passing

Lukas Graham's, You're Not There, Released (2015)

#Coach Takeaways

Mothers are the most important people in your life
for without them you would not exist. #Coach

It's not where you start in life but rather the
journey to your destination completion is
what matters most. #Coach

Rather you're a military service member, business
person or workforce employee good repetitive
behaviors is key to your success. #Coach

Power 2 Live is not a quote it's an intrinsic
motivating force thriving inside of
you providing life. #Coach

If you failed in life, I suggest you don't let that
little setback stop you from being who you
are destined to be. #Coach

Table of Contents

Power 2 Live
Through Obstacles

By Oliver Adams #Coach

The ultimate measure of a man is not where he stands in moments of comfort and convenience, but where he stands at times of challenge and controversy.
—Martin Luther King, Jr.

1

A Mother Knows Best

The streets of South Philadelphia are like other city streets in Los Angeles, New York, Chicago, Atlanta and other major metropolitan areas. They can make or break a young man struggling to find his way. Fortunately for me, my mother Frances Adams was determined to ensure that I would not fall prey to those obstacles. The goals that she set for me inspired me to visualize the life I desired and to ultimately achieve a level of success that few young men in my rugged hometown realized, despite the obstacles.

Television has a way of romanticizing "South Philly" as the supportive village that cheered as Rocky trained for his triumphant victory against Apollo Creed. For me, it was a proving ground. I learned the necessary lessons to survive and thrive with little or no resources. It is said, "self-preservation is the first rule of nature." South Philadelphia engrained in me how to evaluate situations, adapt to my surroundings, and quickly overcome obstacles. As I hustled anything I could sale for a profit on 9th Street of Washington Avenue, I could have easily got into trouble with the law. However, inside of me knowing when to leave a party, when to shut up when speaking out of turn, and picking my fights wisely was some of the Power 2 Live traits warning me while growing up.

Like most teens with nothing to do with all the free time in the world, I rebelled relentlessly against my parents' guidance. What some called "acting out" back then was what modern-day therapists suggest is a routine part of adolescent expression. Armed with a healthy cache of swagger and disregard for authority, I cut classes and hung out with some of the toughest street gangs always looking to get into trouble. I engaged in all types of activities that were in direct contrast to the straight and narrow path that my mother had envisioned for me. Like many others in my age group, it felt liberating and fun to just roll with the crowd. It wasn't long before things got out of hand and landed me into trouble which my mother struggled tirelessly to keep me away from. One day while hanging out with my friends, we stole a car and went joy riding. When we heard the sirens of the police car and saw the red and blue lights flashing things got very scary. I was driving and I didn't know what to do so I hit the gas pedal and that started the chase. After dodging in and out of small streets we finally escaped from the cops and we ditched the car. What a close call, no damage to people or property we all considered ourselves lucky this time? How many times has your mother warned you of certain paths not to take and you did just the opposite? That makes two of us and when people say "momma knows best," you would agree that we should have listened.

In most inner cities across America, young black men were offered few opportunities to avoid trouble and prison was one of the most prevalent and well-traveled roads for many. My mother would entertain no such outcome for me. She was not going to idly watch me voyage down a path of destruction just to end up in prison, or worst dead on the streets. I am not the only person whose mother would do anything humanly possible to protect her children. Desperate to redirect my life and keep me on the straight and narrow, she did what many parents of her generation would do, she whipped my @$$. Now let's be clear, my life was never in danger by getting my @$$ whipped, nor did she leave me with any lifelong emotional scars. Can any of you remember those whippings from your mother but more importantly the love she shared to keep you safe from trouble and harm?

What I do remember, was the pain and disappointment in her eyes each time I got in trouble. It was like someone had defaced her only precious jewel. I couldn't stand to see the look of hope for my future being extinguished in my mother's eyes. With each mistake that I made, I fell further and further away from the version of my life envisioned by my mother. These issues would eventually lead me down a path to nowhere if something didn't change fast. "This stuff must stop" I said to myself; I love my mom too much and the promise to make my mother proud should be my only motivation. It's time to redirect my actions and essentially change my life to fuel my personal Power 2 Live.

Though no one can go back and make a brand new start,
anyone can start from now and make a brand new ending.
—Carl Bard

2

The Recruiter and Hero Proposition

One day on a sunny afternoon, I stumbled into the Army recruiter's office on the outskirts of my neighborhood. I had seen this office hundreds of times before but avoided it religiously. I had heard rumors about the Army and the horrors that war offered. On this day perhaps swayed by my youthful intellectual notions, I was interested in hearing what they had to say. I was no stranger to danger; in fact, I had survived Philadelphia's mean streets but the military was a different environment. In typical and deliberate fashion the army recruiter dazzled me with the prospect of serving my country and a dignified way. Would this make my mother proud by enlisting among the ranks of the thousands of men and women that served before me? He showed me videos with patriotic images and music that subliminally challenged a part within me that longed for greatness. Not only for myself did I want to be like the soldiers in those videos, but also for my mother whose hopes for my future still loomed with promise.

Despite my defiance and rebellion, I had to see what this Hero proposition was all about. This recruiter as if seasoned to speak with troubled teenagers spoke directly to my mindset and gained my attention with his words. "You will be a better man surrounded by soldiers rather than hanging out with street gangs and hustlers." As biting as his words were, they were true. Most mothers raising teenagers in cities struggle to provide for college, especially if they are single head of households. Like many teenagers abroad, finding a way to college would be a responsibility burdened by the young adults who have dreams of success. The recruiter informed me that the Army would pay for my college education if I enlisted. I wondered if making this life changing decision to take my future into my own hands would be the right move and would it make my mother proud of me.

For weeks after leaving the recruiter's office, I considered his words. During one of my final visits to the recruiter's office, I witnessed one of my friends from my neighborhood there with his parents. It was during his swearing in ceremony that I shifted inwardly. He was enlisting and signing up for the Infantry division. Infantry soldiers are the first to fight and have defended this grateful nation for over 200 years. One can only imagine watching as his mother shed tears of joy and being overwhelmed with pride. I wanted that for my mother, she of all people deserved to have a chance to see me "Be All I Could Be." Like many before me and those who committed to serve after me, I decided that this would also become my path to leave the inner city and start my life fresh. Just imagine yourself joining a group of trained experts ready to engage, fight, and defeat the enemy in combat. As young adults, many inner-city youths decided to leave their city streets across America to enlist in the Armed Forces. At that moment, boys became men and families relished with pride and dignity for their choice to stand in the gap to defend this grateful nation. I could hear my mother's voice saying, "You have the Power 2 Live inside and you can be anything you put your mind towards." The Power 2 Live concept would become one of my guiding principles throughout life. That phrase continued to push me toward excellence, even when I felt powerless and alone.

There are no great people in this world, only great challenges, which ordinary people rise to meet.
—William Frederick Halsey, Jr.

3

Preparation Meets the Unknown

The Army prepared me for life in ways that Philadelphia and even my mother could not. My mentality was slowly evolving from a reactive teen with no firm plans for life, to a proactive man always prepared for any situation. To this day, I still wake up thinking about it like it was yesterday... global threats, terrorism, and war.

It was 2:00am when we got the call. An alert of this magnitude would unnerve most people. It seemed so sudden but that's the way we were trained to respond. One of our paratroopers' mantra was "be ready to deploy anywhere in world in 18 hours or less." Preparation and discipline was what we were trained to execute at a moment's notice. Facing H-Hour, the name given to the airborne assault in the Battle of Normandy, meant it is time to go.

As a leader in the United States Army Airborne elite rapid deployment force under the command of the 18th Airborne Corps stationed at Fort Bragg, North Carolina fear took a back seat to preparation. Charged with the responsibility of leading a section of highly motivated and trained soldiers on a key mission, I keenly understood that this wasn't going to be easy, by any stretch. My soldiers were fully rigged for a combat parachute jump into an unknown place and potentially hostile territory. We had trained extensively for this moment and the anticipation was high. I inspected my soldiers' equipment multiple times to ensure they were ready for the mission. The Jumpmasters carefully inspected each soldier's parachute before boarding the C-130 aircraft. This particular aircraft was a massive machine capable of operating from rough dirt strips, was the primary mode of transport for para-dropping troops and equipment into hostile areas.

With a thunderous voice and attention to detail, the Jumpmaster began to yell, "Check Equipment," as each individual jumper sounded off with "OK". I was the last jumper and replied, "All OK Jumpmaster." I do not remember fear as I surveyed the inside of the plane, only the red glow from the blackout lights had my attention. The Air Force loadmasters opened the jump doors and stepped out of the way of the Jumpmaster. The Jumpmaster made a safety check of the door platform and stepped back into the aircraft. He made eye contact with me and yelled, "Stand in the door." I gave my static line to the safety and stepped onto the jump platform. My eyes were fixated on the red jump-caution light at the edge of the door. The light turned green and while slapping me on the butt, the Jumpmaster yelled, "Go"! I hurled myself into the darkness 1,200 feet above the unknown. That moment was symbolic of my life, trusting only what I had learned. As I counted off four seconds, I felt the sudden and welcomed jerk of my parachute opening and the relief of knowing that my drop was safe. As I prepared to land, my feet slammed to the ground and for a fleeting moment I allowed myself to think of the worst-case scenario. Recalling the hours of extensive training that seemed monotonous and boring as we endured them, I was glad preparation was key to our success. Training made my actions automatic and offered little opportunity for failure. Constant preparation and discipline fueled my Power 2 Live while serving as a United States Airborne Paratrooper.

You may encounter many defeats, but you must not be defeated. In fact, it may be necessary to encounter the defeats, so you can know who you are, what you can rise from, how you can still come out of it.
—Maya Angelou

4

Anywhere in the World in 18 Hours

In August 1990, life for me would change once again. The United States Armed Forces launched Operation Desert Shield. Iraq, then ruled by the notorious dictator Saddam Hussein, invaded the citizens and oil fields of its neighboring country, Kuwait. The call for duty was issued for our unit to deploy and prepare for combat if Saddam Hussein did not comply with our Commander and Chief's demand for withdrawal from Kuwait. Our specialized units arrived in South East Asia to a blistering heat index that surged upwards to 120 degrees during the day. I imagined that this was what hell felt like.

After the Coalition Forces led by our brave fighting men and women trained and prepared for months, we waited for the orders to force Iraq out of Kuwait.

Unfortunately, as time passed we found ourselves deployed for an extended time and training began to feel repetitive. The heat was becoming exhaustive and threatened our ability to perform as we trained. Some media analysts suggested that we were at a distinct disadvantage due  to our lack of experience in such extreme hot climates.

During this time, I often recalled how my previous duty stations and growing up in Philadelphia had challenged me. As the remaining services like the Marines and Air Force joined the coalition, we grew in number and adapted to the extreme heat of that region. Just like I had adapted in Philadelphia and plunged myself into the darkness as a paratrooper, this obstacle was no different in my mind.

On February 24, 1991, we changed our mission from Operation Desert Shield to Operation Desert Storm. This is when the decision to take the battle to the enemy was ordered and we collectively led a coalition of the strongest and most fierce armed forces into Kuwait and Iraq to liberate Kuwait and decimate Saddam Hussein Army. Whenever I hear comments of being a proud American, my heart is always reminiscent of what we accomplished against the odds while deployed in Iraq and I am humbled.

Power2Live
Through Obstacles

As we express our gratitude, we must never forget that the highest appreciation is not to utter words, but to live by them.
–John F. Kennedy

5

The Hardest Obstacle to Climb is Death of a Loved One

After my return from Operation Desert Shield/Desert Storm, I was provided leave of absence and headed home to see my family. When I arrived in Philadelphia, I spoke to my mom on the phone around 8pm that evening. "Welcome home Bones (that's what she called me). I missed you so much and can't wait to see you in the morning!" Her tone was warm and loving and assured me that all was well on the home front. I had finally heard the pride in her voice that I sought since my troubled youthful years.

Normally when I took leave, I went directly home first to see my mother but this time it was different. I promised a friend that I would speak to seniors at a local high school. This was the only time in my military service that I did not follow my home visit pattern, which was to go straight home to see my mother. It was also important that I fulfill my promise to speak with the young high school students in my hometown.

My mom was so proud that I had escaped the mean streets of Philadelphia, but even more excited about the fact that I was coming back to inspire those in our community. Knowing my mother was pleased by my choices offered me a sense of fulfillment and peace of mind. It made my visit that much more fulfilling. We couldn't wait to see each other in the morning to catch up on lost time caused by my deployments.

The next morning, I was devastated when I received a call informing me that my mom died of a massive heart attack during the night, she was only 48 years old. She was my biggest supporter and now she was dead. Fear gripped my heart and I didn't know how I was going to make it without her. My spirit was broken but I could still hear her soft voice saying, "You have the Power 2 Live inside of you, Bones."   Her death fueled my ambition to win at any cost because she instilled in my core The Power 2 Live! The very mention of her name seemed to ignite inspiration in my soul as powerful as hearing the roar of the planes I jumped out of as a paratrooper.

In the days following her death, I struggled with the loss of my number one supporter. Resenting daily that she would never get the opportunity to see me again or for my children to sit and talk with their grandmother. Honestly, I was upset with God for taking away my mother, but that's another story for a different time. My peace of mind today comes from knowing that my mother was proud of me, because I lived by her teachings and through the Power 2 Live!

*Do not go where the path may lead,
go instead where there is no path and leave a trail.*
—Ralph Waldo Emerson

6

Live in Overdrive

I made it my mission in life to always challenge myself to exceed my mother's expectations. I worked harder, woke up earlier than my peers to be prepared for the day because taking short cuts was not an option for me. My mother's voice would always echo in my mind, "Did you do your best son?" My response was and will always be, "Yes mom I am doing my best!"

After serving 23 years of successful service in the military, it was time for me to retire. The military taught me to always have a Plan B. Prior to leaving the Army, I had already worked in real estate for over fourteen years. As a soldier, I watched real estate agents dressed in suits with nice cars and I found that alluring. Soldiers would rotate duty stations on average every 3 years and no matter where the job took us we always needed a place to live. After seeing REALTORS drive clients around and explain the home buying process, I decided I wanted to be a REALTOR.

To get started in real estate, I went to college and obtained my real estate license in 1992. After I obtained my

broker's license in 1996, I built a team of eight agents and opened two office locations in Fayetteville NC. While selling real estate, I realized there was also a major obstacle that many soldiers and consumers did not understand and therefore prevented some from purchasing a home. That obstacle was lack of credit worthiness which threatened the dreams of home ownership for so many people. This was such a major disappointment because unscrupulous lenders and creditors held our soldiers' hostage over credit.

That being said, I decided to immerse myself in how to fix credit and eventually became a credit and debt counselor through the Better Business Bureau to address these issues outright. After discussing these credit challenges with other military leaders at Ft. McPherson GA we decided develop a system to foster change in our soldiers' credit scores. As a small team we brain stormed and discussed systems to protect service members and their families from credit predators. The feedback was strategic and it created a system that would help soldiers and anyone who had credit challenges tackle those obstacles. In 2006 Buyers Credit Coach, Inc. www.BuyersCreditCoach.com was birth to help anyone with less than perfect credit, so use this system to get back on the road to credit worthiness and homeownership. This is a gift from the Coach to anyone who want to get back in the game in access their Credit Power 2 Live.

As my story continues, I started serving my country in another way, helping people to live the "American Dream through Home Ownership" and maximize their hard-earned dollars. Assisting homebuyers, sellers, and tenants through real estate provided similar responsibilities to me, like taking care of soldiers. My transactions exceeded countless millions of dollars in value but more importantly, I was imparting the Power 2 Live concept into every one of my clients. Using similar strategies, disciplines and core values adapted from previous life experiences catapulted my real estate career. "Remember opportunities always present themselves to those prepared and ready!"

After coaching countless soldiers and thousands of real estate agents, I arrived at this conclusion… "Knowledge coupled with passion, will provide anyone the edge that will ultimately propel him or her to immeasurable personal success." There are traits that successful people share which set them apart from others. Habits like determination, drive and willpower are game changers in the pursuit of success. These traits are what employers, entrepreneurs, and successful business owners seek to garner when partnering at every level.

During my life's travels, God has always helped me accomplish my small or supersized goals. I have found that by lending a helping hand to others, God has returned that generosity many times over to me and my family. What is even more compelling is that anyone can tap into this power. We all have a story inside of us, regardless of our personal circumstance. The key is to tap into that Power within you and remember that tomorrow isn't promised. We should live purposefully and fully immersed in our dreams.

For me, the battlefield has become the boardroom where I've started several successful businesses and trained thousands of entrepreneurs to identify their Power 2 Live traits and tap into their power source. Empowerment is a word that often is used incorrectly in regular conversation. It indicates authority given to you from an entity or organization, but life itself has provided you the Power 2 Live and the skills to push you to a higher level. Don't sit back and wait to be told what you are supposed to be in life. My mother always told me, "You must rise to life's challenges and embrace your Power 2 Live!"

We are what we repeatedly do.
Excellence, then, is not an act, but a habit.
—Aristotle

7

Encourage Yourself

received my Masters of Business Administration (MBA) Degree and finished at the top of my class through the University of Phoenix (Atlanta). During my degree completion, I was chosen as the Class Speaker in 2015. Looking out into this large stadium with over 14,000 in attendance, I paused and wished I would have seen my mother's smile letting me know that everything was ok. Instead, I felt her in my spirit saying how proud she was of her baby Bones. At that moment, it became clear to me life is worth living and I accept fully my Power 2 Live it to the fullest. To everyone reading this book, remember this quote if you don't remember anything else... "No one can do what you're called to do, no adverse situation, including death, can stop your life's mission." You are an overcomer and obstacle remover! Learn and understand what your life purpose is and then get off your @$$ and go fulfill it!

Regardless of difficult times, the worst of circumstances or the biggest obstacles, view them as opportunities to develop your Power 2 Live. Sometimes those who are least expected to succeed realize the greatest achievements and make others take note for example: Philadelphia Eagles 2nd string quarterback #9 and now Super Bowl LII, MVP, Nick Foles.

Most of you were raised to never let anyone discourage you from the dreams placed inside, whether from a loved one or a senior respected leader. Always challenge yourself to exceed your mothers' expectations, work harder on winning each and every day and things will fall into place, you must have faith! Like many who have succeeded before you, wake up earlier before your peers and prepare yourself for the day. Equip yourself with a Can-Do attitude and a series of motivational rituals as you continued to take leaps of faith daily. As for me, my mom is not here to push me but now my Jumpmaster is God and I'm jumping right into my destiny.

The Power 2 Live runs in your veins, remember options and opportunities always present themselves to those prepared and ready! Develop your habits like getting up early, Dream Big and set goals. Become the best version of yourself so that everyone can see the Power 2 Live inside of you. The world is your playground and it's now up to you to set the standards for yourself and your family. Inspire others to

follow their dreams and never take short cuts. I am proud of you for reading this book and I am hopeful you will exceed your own expectations!

*Obstacles are those frightful things you see when
you take your eyes off your goal.*
—Henry Ford

8

Use God's Power to Overcome

We all know that there are obstacles that we will encounter in life, but people often ask, "Oliver, be more specific, what were some of your obstacles?"

This book was designed to help you wake up and take action. When you think about life, the obstacles and challenges that may be hindering you in your life, it's easy to just lay dormant and let life happen to you rather than going after what you want. Too often people fall prey to distractions that keep them stuck. The bad news is that our attention is often challenged by friends, work schedules, and the most dreaded social media notifications. Therefore staying focused is often harder now than ever before.

As I begin to reflect about obstacles that challenged me over the years, I think about **8 obstacles** that could have caused me to fail horribly:

1. Discord - A lack of harmony between persons or things. I have encountered situations that were dysfunctional and I had to decide to separate myself from the confusion. You may add a few of your own.

2. Jealousy - Resentment against a person enjoying success. I know there were people who resented me and did not want to see me succeed. My success made them feel less than, but if I was going to succeed, I couldn't focus on haters.

3. Rage - Full of rage; furious. I met people and encountered folks that had anger that they wanted to propel towards me. Rage is devastating and it do not care who are the victims, stay clear of this trait.

4. Selfishness - Caring only for oneself; concerned primarily with one's own interests, benefits and welfare regardless of others. Many people only care about themselves, but no one does anything great alone. In order for you to succeed you must be willing to give freely at times and do so out of humility.

5. Ambition without Direction – Having a strong desire and determination to succeed, but not knowing how to succeed. So many people are excited and passionate about movement, rather than progress. This leaves them running in circles lacking a destination or a plan to get there.

6. Dissension - disagreement that leads to discord. A difference of opinion is normal, but can also lead to confusion and a disconnect that place a wedge in a potentially valuable relationship.

7. Envy - A feeling of discontent or resentfulness of someone else's possessions, qualities, or luck. Many people I encountered were resentful of what I had accomplished and they will be the same towards you if you're not mindful. If your treated with hostility or negativity this could be the reason.

8. Strife - Angry or a disagreement over fundamental issues creates conflict. I have been in situations that were consistently hostile and the behavior showed me that it would be hard for me to succeed while remaining, so I had to separate myself. It's that simple, "if you can't beat them leave them!" #Coach

These were eight (8) of the challenges that I had to overcome, they showed up in almost every area in my life and you will not be immune from them either. This was not a physical challenge but rather a fight of values and principles. Concepts like institutional racism

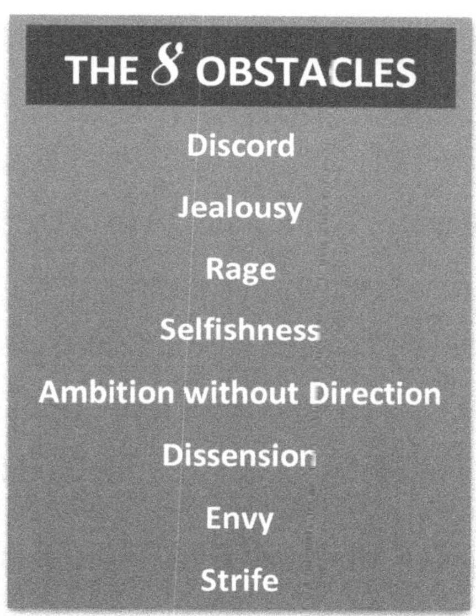

was too big for me to challenge at my level. After discovering that racism and hatred resided in certain people I took a deeper dive into those behaviors and challenged the root source. Certain people gravitate to obvious differences and choose not to participate in universal spiritual principles as you will soon see in this book.

Knowing all that I know now, if I had to refer to a scripture, I would go to the book of Galatians, the 5th chapter and 20th verse. Here are the universal principals that I mentioned. I am in no way advocating that I'm a preacher, but this is how I overcame behaviors and attitudes that was beyond my depth. Many mothers sacrificed much to help their children know what is important in life and how to overcome obstacles at different levels. Ground yourselves and be patient when you feel the pressures of life. Be gentle at times, when you want to be forceful. Face your obstacles by being smart but also stern and direct as you take each step towards your Power 2 Live!

One obstacle you must avoid is allowing people to take advantage of you and be sure your willing to do whatever it takes to stay true to yourself! As soon as you catch wind that someone is trying to abuse or take advantage of you, shut it down! If you know something is wrong with a situation, you may feel the urge to push back. When you push back give it some deep thought first, next try to isolate where it's coming from. The Coach recommends one way to combat this obstacle, grab your Bible and find a quiet place to read Galatians, 5th chapter 22nd – 23rd verse, which says ***"But the fruit of the Spirit is love, joy, peace, forbearance, kindness, goodness, faithfulness, gentleness and self-control. Against such things there is No Law."***

Simply put, identify the trait or the root of the problem and don't try to take a bat and swing at every pitch that is thrown at you. Pull out the one trait and deal with it using the rules already identified in God's Bible to combat that obstacle. That's how I had the power to overcome and that is what I recommend to you.

USE GOD'S POWER TO OVERCOME

Love, joy, peace, forbearance, kindness, goodness, faithfulness, gentleness and self-control.

The message of "Power 2 Live Through Obstacles" resurrects lost and unrealized dreams by striking the match of hope coupled with the energy of accountability.

—Vicky Samuel

9

Behaviors and Actions Count

As you read through this book, you'll find one central theme that I concentrate on. From the time I was a kid to adulthood I concentrated on behaviors. I believe that focusing on peoples' behaviors is the way to affect change. It's too difficult to let the whirlwind of perceptions dictate who a person is inside.

In life, observing different personal attributes is important in the process of understanding behaviors. The chess players in society choose different tactics to deal with race, religion and the noise of politics. They rather deal with people actions and what they observe, because their actions always show the truth of who a person is and what they subscribe to in life. As I close this story line I want to share with you the rewards of staying focused and accessing your Power 2 Live after your storms have passed.

Actions speak louder than words, I used positive behavior traits to become a productivity coach, systems restructuring mentor and focus driven educator to propel business owners to accept the best systems for their businesses. That being said, I am now a quantifiable coach who helps people get out of their own way and make it to their goals and destiny.

My quest for excellence in real estate took me from being a chairman of a membership committee at my local board to becoming the President of my Board of REALTORS® in the year 2016. Our board happened to be one of the largest Boards in the State of Georgia, but that still wasn't enough so I turned my efforts toward real estate agents productivity. Wrapping my mind around the concept of production and REALTORS® growth being my number #1 goal; it was not just from a practitioner viewpoint but the question was how do you get others to master the trade of real estate and make money to feed their families? They say what you attract most shows up and did it show up through business collaborations. My good friend Toya Davis-Stevenson, Team Leader at one of Atlanta's Keller William Realty franchises offered me an opportunity to coach her agents to success. As a productivity coach I slowly and methodically pushed agents towards their success using proven system and tools. Toya, is a very smart and energetic woman with a vision for her team. I learned so much under her leadership and for that I will be forever grateful for her giving me the opportunity to coach.

In early 2016, I met a man by the name of Kevin Levent, Owner and CEO of Better Homes and Gardens Real Estate Metro Brokers and he saw something special in me. During a Broker's Council meeting on the South Side of Metro Atlanta where I was the host moderator, Kevin observed attributes that he concluded would be good for his large real estate firm of over 2,200 agents and he approached me with a mind-blowing opportunity.

Better Homes and Gardens Real Estate Metro Brokers was located throughout the state with over 26 offices, this position would stretch me but I was up to the challenge. After two lunches and little convincing, I knew this would be a perfect fit. Kevin advocated the use of systems for agents' success and operated with such structure that it reminded me of my days in the military. Metro Brokers used technology and platforms to make sure that their real estate agents did not have to skimmer to get the resources they needed to succeed. This was nothing short of a Win-Win for me as it related to my endeavor to become the best real estate coach ever. A quote from Malcolm Gladwell book Outliers, A Story of Success came to mind "Practice isn't the thing you do once you're good. It's the thing you do that makes you good." Equipped with well over 10,000 hours of coaching and mentoring garnered over my tenure in real estate for 27 years and service in the military for 23 years it was time for me to give back to my collective profession. Coaching allowed me to focus on adding value to REALTORS® and small business owners using my greatest asset or super power of sorts. That power is helping others reach their goals personal business goals. I committed myself totally to the concept of Productivity and Craig McClelland, COO of Better Homes and Gardens Real Estate Metro Brokers gave me some simple guidance. He said, "Oliver let us help you systemize what you do. You already have the inspiration, motivation and the skill sets, you need to think bigger and we can help you with that proposition?" Your challenge for Metro Brokers is to help our agents get to the next deal fast. In addition, Craig said, "Let's coach our agents to cap in five months or less." Those words resonated with me, so I accepted the challenge and never looked back.

For the last two years, I have been one of the Business Coaches for Metro Brokers, coaching agents to build their business using our support staff and training classes. My growth as a coach has led me to help create more million dollars producers than I could have ever fathomed doing it alone. Metro Brokers assist agents in so many ways by promoting their motto and tag line of "In Business for Yourself, Not by Yourself."

This is how I continued to transfer the Power 2 Live into REALTORS® through motivation, inspiration and hard work.

My challenge to everyone that I coach is to exceed your goals by focusing on what you can do now and stick to your game plan. Everyone is a winner if they give 110% of themselves to their dreams and business goals. Anything short of hard work and use of the Power 2 Live concept can result in mediocrity.

Lastly, there are those who ask... Coach did you have any success stories from your mentors growing up? My response is Yes, recently I had an opportunity to celebrate a man that showed me how to become a fisher of men. He was one of the key people in the village that was created for protection of young teens in my neighborhood. This village helped me navigate the tough streets of South Philadelphia. Kevin Washington who was recently selected as the President and CEO of the YMCA of America and he was my guide.

It was at the Christian Street YMCA in Philadelphia where I first met Kevin. This man influenced my life when I was only 16 years old. He helped mold me as my youth mentor along with others in the neighborhood. He guided me as my counselor and provided opportunities through sports, organized events and community involvement. I remember Kevin saying, "I believe all young folks are at risk no matter where they live. It's the communities' responsibility to ensure that the bridge from adolescence to adulthood is the foundation on which we stand."

It was people like Kevin as well as my mother who paved the way for my success. Today, encourage all those who have a heart of compassion to help people through obstacles and become the new story line. Be proud of your hard work and know that it is not in vain. Every day as you go into your communities to share your passion, remember that transformational moments happen daily. I wish for you and all those who have welcomed the Power 2 Live to follow your dreams until they are achieved! **#COACH**

CPSIA information can be obtained
at www.ICGtesting.com
Printed in the USA
LVHW021658170720
660993LV00011B/564